L. LUIS LÓPEZ

MUSINGS OF A BARRIO SACK BOY

In English, Spanish, and Spanglish

For Cassandra
Con mucho cariño
L. Luis López
11/15/2009

Farolito Press

Grand Junction, Colorado

i

ISBN 0-9679844-0-8
Library of Congress Catalog Card No. 00-132264

Cover by Andrew Gruner
Photo on cover: Ben Barreras

Farolito Press
P.O. Box 60003
Grand Junction, Colorado 81506

for

Fred and Annie Nigro

Ben and Irene Barreras

y

Para mi Barrio

ACKNOWLEDGMENTS

Encounter with La Llorona upon His Return from Harvard, *The Americas Review*

Father Dan, *Karamu*

Felina, *The Americas Review, from Día de Visitaciones (a play)*

From a Ten Year Old Sack Boy, *Karamu*

Images of San Luis, *Geography of Hope, From the Heart*

Nehi Strawberry Down-and-Away, *Fan: A Baseball Magazine, Geography of Hope*

Niño, *The Americas Review, from Día de Visitaciones (a play)*

only now I realize, *From the Heart*

Santos, *from Día de Visitaciones (a play)*

Solomón, *The New Mexico Journal, The Americas Review, from Día de Visitaciones (a play)*

To a Coal Miner, *Pinyon, Geography of Hope*

Tomás, *Geography of Hope, The Americas Review, from Día de Visitaciones (a play)*

v

Table of Contents

INTRODUCTION

I grew up in an Albuquerque neighborhood with both the grocery store and the church in my blood. At a very young age, about seven or eight, I began helping stock, sweep, clean, deliver, and on occasion check customers at the counter. I worked at Fred's Grocery and, when Ben bought out Fred, at Ben's Grocery until I was about sixteen years old. At that time, I began working at the neighborhood service station. These jobs allowed me to meet the neighborhood. At the grocery store I witnessed a parade of customers that now manifest themselves in my poems and plays. What I find in my memory banks are the salient features of each character and situation--a cartoonist emphasizing the prominent. The prominent expresses itself as humor and sorrow, so the poems are either funny or sad, oftentimes both.

The Catholic Church was just across the street from the grocery store. Since our lives were governed by the liturgical cycle and since so many in the neighborhood were Catholic, I was able to see these same customers in a religious context. Little by little, I also got to know them in other contexts. I began to realize that the person I knew at the grocery store was not necessarily the same person I saw at church, or at the service station, or at his or her home. This led to some humorous and to some sad conclusions about people in general.

In my mind, the church and neighborhood were the same, so I was curious and actually concerned about those who were not Catholic. I worried if they would be saved, so I prayed for them. Their situation didn't seem to bother them; and, of course, as I grew older this curiosity and concern gradually disappeared. Now I look back and find my concerns humorous. In addition, I thought that everyone spoke both English and Spanish, so I was concerned about those that didn't. Little by little I learned that one should converse in one of three languages: English, a formal Spanish spoken at home and among older adults, and a mixture of English and Spanish used among my friends and in the bantering that went on at the grocery store. One just learned to adapt. Today, Spanglish is very common among second, third, and even fourth generation Hispanics of the Southwest.

When I began to think myself a poet (some time in my thirties),
I was bothered by the fact that many journal, magazine, and
anthology editors thought my poetry silly since some were
written in Spanglish. Because the language of poetry reflects
the poet and the people the poet writes about, I felt frustrated. I
tried to write some of the Spanglish poems in straight English
or Spanish, but they lost their flavor. They became different
poems. I finally realized that each poem writes itself. An
English poem is English, a Spanish poem is Spanish, and a
Spanglish poem is Spanglish. For that reason, this volume
contains all three. Editors are more open to Spanglish poems
now than they were in the 1960's, 70's, or 80's. In fact, there
are some attempts to publish anthologies in mixed code. As far
as I know, none have been completed. Because I do not use
Spanish on a day to day basis any longer, the reader will realize
that English has become dominant. I write much better in
English than in Spanish, but I love to write poems in Spanish,
so I have included my attempts in this volume.

I feel that I have brought the memory of many of the
people in my neighborhood to life through these poems. A
Spanish word for neighborhood is *barrio*. Today this word
seems to designate a poor Hispanic neighborhood, but that is
not necessarily the case. My barrio, which we simply called
South Broadway, was a mixture of many economic levels and
many types of people. All appear in these poems. I feel the
poems reflect life both in their subtle humor and in their
poignant expression of sorrow.

L. Luis López

From a Ten Year Old Sack Boy

Señora Mendoza, you're wondering why
I can't take my eyes from you. You
disapprove of where I look. But how
can I help it when you come into the store
dressed in that low-cut blouse with
Christ on the cross hanging on a gold
chain between what you disapprove I see?

Father Dan

assistant pastor
at the Immaculate Conception
put in charge
of parish teens
because he was more
our age
and spoke our language

one evening in May
month of Mary
he gave a sermon
to the youth
of the Legion of Mary
on the dangers of French kissing

which
I didn't know
anything about until then

only now I realize

> your Radiola recording of The Amos 'n' Andy Show
> brought to mind those winter evenings
> when Mom and Dad sat on the couch in the dark
> and you and I lay beside the coal-burning stove
> > four of us
>
> lost in a succession of half-hour worlds
> > each of us
>
> chuckling at Fibber McGee's clattering tumble
> at Charlie's maneuvering Bergen
> snickering with Baby Snooks
> laughing at the Schnozz at Digger's "I'll be shoveling off"
> and patiently accompanying Benny to lock
> after rusting lock down basement stairs
> to the ancient vault holding his famous hoard
> > only now I realize
>
> it is not so much those half-hour worlds
> that move me as the closeness we shared
> in the dim light of the Philco dial and the
> slow red glow of her Camel and his Chesterfield

Images of San Luis

Often of late
And far from this poor
Tin-roofed-made-to-look-like adobe church
I see a votive candle burn low in a red glass

Sole illumination in this dark corner
Of a chipped plaster image
Of San Luis de Gonzaga
Church patron
Standing two feet high
Yellowing surplice over faded black cassock

Eyes downcast, seeking heaven

This is where my father stood to make his peace
When times were difficult
To ask forgiveness of stubborn sin through his namesake

And where I now stand
Drawn from afar to make my difficult peace
With the memory
Of his tobacco smell and whiskey breath

Gloria

Gloria in Excelsis Deo . . .

Sonya sang it so sweetly
Martha was melodious
Betty's voice was beautiful
Rita was exact
Lydia loud
Gloria always out of tune
But one Sunday
Gloria lost her voice

. . . et in terra pax hominibus

buscando la gloria eterna

cada día una viejita madruga
y vestida de negro
camina
por la calle hacia la iglesia
para oír la sagrada misa
rezar por su alma
ganar la gloria eterna

esta mañana
en un arbol junto
a la iglesia
un gusano
color de gris
camina
por ramo hacia hojas sobrasas
donde
piensa envolverse en capullo
para ganar
la gloria de ser mariposa

it is morning (akin to "buscando")

it is morning
a poor black-shawled woman
edges along the roadside
toward Mass
intent on earning eternal glory

in a tree by the church
a caterpillar
edges along a branch
toward lush leaves
cocoon
intent on butterfly glory

Adán

They don't let Adán drink his vino
at La Paloma anymore.
The cantinero told him so.
Even la jura.
But he can buy a pint and take it home.

He's not allowed to drink there either.
His wife told him so.
And not at his next door neighbor's,
nor at his friend's.

He has to drink en otro lugar.

¿Y porqué?

Porque cuando he drinks his vino,
he becomes smart,
a master at argument,
el mismo diablo,
ojos on fire, doubled fists looking
for chingazos,
or he becomes a clown, un payazo.

Con cariño, he puts the pint
in his back bolsa
and heads to his special drinking place
where he can enjoy his traguitos,
un lugar along the acequia
where he can either argue con los pájaros,
pelear con los bushes,
or tell jokes to the feathers
and the hojas sitting on the branches.

But someone is there.
Un couple making out in his drinking
place. So he takes un traguito
and goes to his other place,
bajo el puente. Pero he takes
another traguito, un slug, and so emerges
the clown, the one who loves to make

8

la gente laugh. So he makes his journey
to the puente seem
dangerous by gulping down tres más.

Putting the pint, otra vez con cariño,
in this back bolsa,
he imagines dancing on a tight rope,
three stories up,
parasol en la mano,
while actually balancing along a foot-wide
path, brown water gushing a warning
of quick death on one side,
broken glass and rusting botes threatening
deep gashes
were he to slip and tumble down the other.

Left foot on the rope,
la mano izquierda holding the parasol,
he teeters,
then falls,
not into the acequia,
not onto the rusting botes or on broken glass,
but smack on this butt,
the pint splintering, gashing, puncturing,
disinfecting-all al mismo tiempo.

In his clown mind se acuerda de ese otro
Adán, in English, Adam,
the one who wounded todo el mundo
con un bite de la apple
while, according to the priest,
as Adán understands it,
producing Jesucristo on the cross as antiseptic.

Ese Adam no era payaso.
He wasn't no clown.

"Too bad," Adán says to that other Adam
as he rises and pulls down his pants
to examine his wounds,
"If you had been a clown,
then God would not have taken you so seriously."

Telemo

Red headband and a pack of Camels folded
into sleeve of sweaty T-shirt mark him macho,
but at the rosary lagrimas well into his eyes as
his mother's face swims at him from the coffin
through steamy air and rise and fall of prayer.
And as if at a fish bowl glass, her lips form
the words, "Ruega por mí Telemo, ahora y en
la hora de mi muerte," until face and prayer recede
and he begins to fear words that follow funeral
prayer, "I'm sorry. Lo siento mucho. If I can be
of any help. Me acuerdo cuando tu mamá . . .
Dios te ayude. It's for the best. Lupe . . . mujer
de paciencia." Words that drain as they did
cuando Odiséo, su papá, deserted la familia
for Los Ángeles. Overwhelming sorrow escapes
Telemo's lips, a sorrow echoed in the deep sigh
of a man standing next to him, un vagamundo,
unnoticed until now, who touches his sleeve,
points to the pack of Camels y en voz conocido
ruega, "Telemo, por favor, un frajo para Odiséo.

Mario Martínez

No matter what Mario Martinez tried en la vida,
He saw himself standing at the back door,
Hat in hand. That's what he believed about himself.
Not good enough for the front door. Apologetic,
Con verguenza, siempre esperando to be recognized,
To be hired, to be invited. In Spanish esperando
Means hoping as well as waiting, and that was
Mario-hoping-waiting. ¡Ay Dios! A life
Can go by like that. And in the case of Mario,
It did. This morning he is waiting at the church
To be buried, pero nadie está allí except the priest
And the altar boys. Espera, hat in hand, for Dios.

Solomón

Solomón lay
face down on a narrow
embankment between bosque and river,
eyes closed to the sunset.
He could see
his body,
drunk, drug-plagued,
burdened with its heavy soul,
drag its feet
through the burning afternoon,
stumble over roots
and rotting logs
as it shuffled
upstream
beside the Rio Grande's
torrential late spring rush
to the sea.

It was of a mind
to let itself
join the torrent
until it saw
a narrow place
beneath the shimmering silver leaves
and protecting thorns
of a Russian Olive.

There it could
lie down
and brood
about how it came
to brother those
who haunted these banks,
joined those who carried their shame
in brown paper bags,
talked to the river,

expressed grandiose solutions
to minor problems,
here and there a sister
of the bottle.

In this protected place
beneath
the Russian Olive,
he relived
those long nights
in his study
when sips from the bottle stimulated
creation-poem, short story,
insightful essay-and
saw how the sips
slowly hardened his alert
soul, making it
heavy, leaden, inert.

Still prone,
he opened his eyes
and watched
the muddy torrent
slowly change to blood
as it reflected
the red and purple fumes
that hovered
over the nearby city's
depleting day.

Suddenly,
the sun's slanting rays
glanced off the
Great River's back
and drove like hurled spears
through his open eyes
and broke
into the back of his head.
The pain left him senseless.

He dreamt
of being awakened
by three books
flapping noisily
in the branches above him.
When the books
sensed he was awake,
one left the trio
and flew out over the river
where it flapped
so wildly
that all of its words
shook loose
from its pages
and fell into
the red torrent
where they were swept
away to the distant sea.
Empty of words,
the book disappeared
into the bosque
on the opposite shore.

He began to wonder
about the shaken words
when the second book
flapped violently
and repeated the act.

When the third book
started its flight,
he shouted
and reached through the silver
leaves to grab it.
He recoiled
as puncturing thorns
tore into hand and arm.
With astonished sorrow
he watched
the third book
shake free its words
and disappear
into the bosque

14

In grief he awoke
and sat and wondered
what loss
he had witnessed-
what story,
what well-wrought poem,
what message from author
was shaken from
those now blank pages
and rushed to oblivion.

In mind
Solomón was moved
to record this loss.

Word,
and image,
and turn of phrase
danced deftly
from head to heart to soul.
Anxious expectation
of polishing,
finishing,
surged through his being.
His own book
would tell
the story of loss.

Celebrate!
Celebrate with wine!
Find a brother of the bottle
willing to share his joy!

He did.

He sipped
at the red liquid
until it warmed its way

from heart
to head
and there blurred
word, image, phrase.

Dimly
he could see
his own book
flapping wildly over the river,
words falling,
as his own mind
rushed to oblivion.

Mr. Evans

Conductor on the Super Chief
"colored man"
my mom used to say

super neat in blue
complete with pocket watch
gold chain
hanging over belly

ticket punch
in right coat pocket

shiny shoes

glasses
little rectangles
halfway
down his nose

bachelor

brought us
a heaping platter
of his Independence Day
barbecue
ribs and chicken
enough for seven
at two p.m.
on the dot
every Fourth of July

which we ate
washed
then returned on September 16
Grito de Dolores
Mexican Independence Day

with one scoop of refried beans
one tortilla
one enchilada

one tamale
one taco
one chile relleno
one sopaipilla
a bowl of red chile
and
one
apricot
empanada for dessert

since he was only . . .

Mr. Baca

fireman
not as neat
as Mr. Evans in blue

drove a bright-red truck
sirens blaring
all
through the night

Mrs. Baca
said "Shhh!" in an angry way
when we played
near their bedroom window
morning
noon
or evening

so when I complained
to my dad
about her getting mad
he told me to tell her to tell
Mr. Baca
not to be so loud
when he drove
on our street at night
when we slept

since there were
no cars on the road anyway

El Señor Rodríguez

in Post Office gray

drove us crazy
with complaints
about dogs that bark and bark
and bark
when he delivers the mail

my grandma finally
said

"Señor Rodríguez
you shouldn't complain
since dogs
bark and bark and bark
at our cat
and she don't
even deliver the U.S. Mail"

Mr. Loftus

gringo who spoke
Spanish
better than the Spanish
in our
neighborhood

ex-cowboy
operated a crane
for the Santa Fe Railroad

changed into cowboy
hat and boots
when he got home

pitched horseshoes
in his yard
and practiced
roping
with us kids as cows

but said
"It's really hard
to make

good cows

out of bad donkeys"

Mr. Hutchinson

in painter's cap and overalls

truck and ladders and buckets and tarp
speckled like trout
came over to paint our kitchen

I still can't believe
how fast he worked
   or how much he talked
      or how much he whistled
         or how much he sang

when he finished
gramma paid him right away
and didn't complain about the spots
he missed
   on the ceiling
      on the walls
like she always did with me

I guess because I never got paid

El Señor Dunworth

shoe repair man in apron brown
fixed my shoes for free
when he saw
I had stuffed bits of old linoleum
in each shoe
to keep my feet from showing through

how he loved to talk about the coal mines
in Utah
Colorado
and New Mexico
about being a welder in San Francisco

but most of all
he loved to tease the priest

one day he said to Father O'Grady

my shop is holier
than your church
because I sell people new soles
and because all the tongues
in my shop
except mine
practice the holy vow of silence

Mr. Dow

delivered the daily paper
in his model T

first light of morning

last light of evening

wore blue-striped overalls
over
orange long johns

delivered to hundreds
of houses
this side
half-a-hundred that side
of the track

one day he took me

I asked

"How do you remember
which
houses get what papers?"

he answered

"I just
remember the ones that don't!"

Mr. Gutiérrez

expert grease monkey
in Texaco cap
spent
all day looking up at bottoms
of cars
on the hydraulic jack

wore his Air Force cap
on holidays
dedicated to war
and
on the day
he was shot down over France

bottom gunner on a B-29

told a woman he had bailed out
upside down
scars on his head to prove it

told the same woman
when he was servicing her car
that he was a good grease monkey
because
he was trained to shoot from the bottom

that's the day Mr. Teofilo Gutiérrez was fired

Santos

Puffing and chewing on a Swisher Sweet,
Santos limped painfully from meat block
To meat counter, meat counter to meat block.
"Football injury," he mumbled at my questioning
Stare-my first day as sack boy and sweeper.
Stabbing a price tag into a pan of ground beef
Edged with green plastic for appetizing display,
He complained, "I scored four *pinche* touchdowns
Against them Bulldoggies and we still got beat."
Placing his cigar on the edge of the meat block,
He picked up his Batman and Robin comic book,
Said, "Break!" and disappeared into the bathroom.

Santos seldom talked football. He joked, teased,
Played pranks, laughed, sang, danced-Harry James
Often accompanied him via the Zenith radio
As he sawed a shoulder roast or sliced bologna.
One day he shook a pan of liver and sang, "I don
Wanner, you can haver, she's too fat for me," then
Joked about Jello for dessert while shaking his flat
Bottom and middle age belly. "I'm gonna die
Laughing," he said as he stamped his foot on the
Sawdust floor. Pain shot through his leg.
"Son of a *gon*!" he cursed through clenched teeth.
A special remedy kept in a bottle behind the
Meat block, *un traguito*, he called it, helped
To ease the crippling agony. "Ahhhh!" he smiled.

I remember how Santos loved to put on his Joker
Face to wait on the lovely ladies. One day he told
A pretty newly wed to buy a pound of chicken brains.
"They're on sale for ten dollars a half pound," he
Informed her. "And when you get pregnant, eat them
With scrambled eggs and tortillas for breakfast.
They'll make your baby smart!" "Oh, sí," she giggled.
"Like me," he added and laughed as he pointed
A twirling index finger at his head. The whole store
Heard him. "Even the rooster heads are good," he said
As he pointed at me. Luis collects them, takes out the
Tonsils, and cooks them with chili. He thinks they will

Help him to sing like ese Caruso in the opera. My face
Became a beet as he laughed and the whole store
Laughed with him. "*Hijo*, that Santos!" people said.

Another day Santos put on his Riddler's face and asked
A customer, "Hey, Mrs. Green, you're a teacher, aren't
You?" "Yes, Santos," she said. "Do you know how
A steak is like a knight in shining armor?" "No, I don't,
Santos," she answered. "Tell me." Santos pulled
Proudly on his apron straps, then pointed to a painting
Of a knight on a horse on the wall above the radio.
"That's Sir Lancelot." Then holding up a fresh cut steak
For her to inspect, added, "This, my lady, is Sir Loin!"

That same day, Santos asked me to ask *la viejita* Rufina
What she had in the brown bag she kept taking out of her
Large canvas purse. "No," I said. "She'll get mad at me."
"*Mira*," he said. "I'll ask her. *Oye*, Rufina, what do you
Have in the bag you keep taking out of your purse?"
"*No te importa*," she said. "But if you really want to know,
It's my medicine, Santos." "Tell me, Rufina," Santos
Went on, "is it true that you drank so much Thunderbird
That when your baby was born it looked like an eagle?"
"Not as bad as you, Santos. When you get married,
Your poor wife will have an Old Crow," she cackled
With joy. "*¡Palo!* You got me with that one, Rufina!"
Santos roared, and he repeated her answer over and over.

Smelling of after shave lotion and a Swisher Sweet,
Santos danced into the store. "Where is she?
Where's Cat Woman? I want to dance." "She's in
The meat market," I went along. "Thank you, Luis."
He bowed and waltzed to the back of the store where
He put on a clean white apron, turned on the radio,
Bowed to a leg of mutton on the meat block, and said
"Will you join me in 'Pennsylvania 6-5000' my lady?"
With leg in arm he whirled and whirled behind the
Meat counter to trombones, clarinets, and trumpets
Until his own legs buckled and he fell smack on the
Floor, the leg of mutton swinging out on its hoof,
Hung there as if ready to be pulled back, then landed
Slap on the meat block and lay there patiently

As Santos suppressed a cry and reached for the
Remedy that would relieve the throbbing pain.
"My apologies," he said to the lady on the meat block.

"A wife can't stand to have a happy man," Santos
Announced one day. "That's why I'll never tie the knot."
But he did admit he fancied the slightly *gorditas* to
The lean ones. Then speaking more to the meat he
Was cutting than to me or his customers, he added,
"Not to change the subject, but the other day I went
To the university to register to be a doctor. They
Kicked me out when I told them I was a butcher!"
He laughed, but it wasn't his old laugh, and I noticed
He was making more and more trips to his "*traguitos*"
Behind the meat block. "A little nip will make me
Hip," he'd giggle and sing between pulls from the bottle.

This morning, as I was spreading fresh sawdust on the
Meat market floor, Santos started chuckling to himself
As he trimmed fat from a steak. He mumbled something
About a half-back in a T-bone formation. He carefully
Arranged the steaks, placed them in the meat counter,
Then cleaned the block. Taking chickens from the cooler,
He began to clean them. "The day I scored those four
Touchdowns, they stopped calling me chicken legs."
His brows furrowed as he picked out a chicken, chopped
Off a wing, then holding the wing before his eyes,
Snapped it in two. Tears glistened as he opened his eyes
And as he reached behind the block for the remedy.
The bottle was empty. He noticed I was watching.
He looked at the empty bottle, then he looked back at me.
His face slowly became the Joker's as he said, "Luis.
Mira. It's a good thing. The *traguitos* that come
In this bottle are not good for the tonsils." With that,
He laughed like his own self then limped to the radio
Where Harry James was waiting to accompany him on a
Sawdust stage behind the meat counter at Fred's Grocery.

La Señal de la Cruz

Crespo managed con un brazo, el derecho,
El izquierdo lost en un accidente,
Pero he never let the loss dissuade him.
That trait made me almost do it in my pants
More than once in our long acquaintance.

Crespo raised gallinas. He killed them
And plucked them and cut them for the stores
To sell. One day I . . . he decided to show me!

He took me to the gallinero, eyed one, raised
His left eyebrow at it, grabbed it by the neck,
Twisted it over his head like a helicopter
Until he heard or felt the snap, then in a blur
Dropped it on the stump, grabbed the axe
Standing handle up against the stump
And arced it like a comet on its neck, severed
Head and body going off in different directions.
With that he turned to me, eyed me, raised
His left eyebrow at me-I ran como el diablo
Father Dan talked about in church who saw
Jesus and didn't want to be turned into a pig.

Hijo, ese Crespo, he scared everybody.

He owned a Chevrolet pickup with the gears
On the floor. Una noche I drove with him
From Albuquerque to Santa Fe. When he had
To change gears, he let go of the steering wheel,
His left foot went down on the cloche, he made
La señal de la cruz, he switched gears, he made
Another señal de la cruz as his left foot lifted
From the cloche, then he returned his hand to
The steering wheel—all before I could say
"Jesús, María, y José!" And I'm still alive!

I never drove with Crespo again. ¡Hijo!
What if he had lost his right arm instead?

Fred

greeted customers
in apron fresh
as he
unlocked the doors
at seven in the morning

carried a bag
of jokes
in his head for the day

said

the neighborhood
would die
of sadness and starvation
without him

one morning
the tiny child of a customer
who hadn't paid his bill
in three months
handed him a note

Fred huffed a breath
of anger
but put a quart of milk
and
a box of Wheaties in a paper sack

handed it to the child

smiled

said

"Tell your dad 'Don't be such a stranger.'"

Annie

She was best at miracles
        a saint before her time

Every time she checked
and sacked the groceries
        she caused a candy bar
        a pack of gum
        or a toy
to appear in the sack
one for each child
by the time
parents unpacked the groceries at home

This never happened when
        Fred
        or Ben
        or Lupe
        or Santos
checked and sacked the groceries

We need to put Annie in the Litanies

Tell the priest
        to tell the monsignor
        to tell the bishop
        to tell the archbishop
        to tell the Pope
to skip the process of beatification
and
to add Annie to the list

St. Annie of the Store, "Ora pro nobis."

Milagro entre Comestibles (Akin to "Annie")

mujer de milagros la esposa
del dueño
cada vez que ella ensacaba
los comestibles
aparacía
    un dulce
    un chicle
    o un juguete
en el saco
uno para cada niño
cuando los padres
sacaban los comestibles en casa

eso nunca ocurría
cuando ensacaba
    Lupe
    o Santos
    of Fred
    o Ben

dile al sacerdote
    que le diga al monsignor
    que le diga al obispo
    que le diga al arzobispo
    que le diga al Papá

que añade esta mujer de milagros
viva
a la lista de santos y santas

"¡Santa Annie, ruega por nosotros!"

Back Then

The open pack lying on the cash register
era para el owner if la jura came to ask.
"You aren't supposed to sell one cigarro
at a time," they used to say. "It's against
the law!" Cigarettes cost ten centavos
a pack of twenty back then, but who
could afford a dime much less spare one?
Pero si tuvieras un penny to your name,
you could put it on the back steps of the
store, heads up, pull the cordón tied to
la campanita on the screen door, "Ding!
Ding!" And yell, "¡Órale, José, aquí esta
el señor Lincoln. Quiere entrar!" Or
in English if the owner wasn't there, "Hey!
Lincoln's home!" Then walk real slow
To the front of the store to find que
Alguien had left one cigarro on the window
Ledge just below the LSMFT (Lucky Strike
Means Find Tobacco) sign.
At the back, someone had let Lincoln in.

Genes

I

"De tal palo tal astilla," Abuelita rasped
after mi jefito bolted down a fourth tequila
and turned on me about "que duro era
in the olden days." I had just asked about
a new pair of shoes for my eighth grade.
"I had one pair, and I walked descalzo
to school to save them," he boasted.
then came the "cinco millas....the cinco feet
de nieve"....and the usual "up hill both ways"
as he left the room con un definite, "No!"
"No way was I going to be an astilla from
mi jefito's palo," I lectured Abuelita.
"And why can't you say a 'chip off the old
block' like the teacher says at school?"

II

Ayer I came home to find mi'jita with big
tears as she set the table for supper.
"¿Qué pasa, mi'jita?" I asked. "Mom said
I have to take the bus to school," she sobbed.
"Did you let that pendejo boyfriend of yours
drive again?" I demanded. "But I have to get
up at six to catch...." "Six?" I interrupted.
"When I was in school, I had to get up at 4:30
to catch the bus a mile away. Now those
luxury liners pick you up aquí in front
of the house! Hijo, you kids nowadays!"
And I turned to get a cerveza from the kitchen.
"A sheep off the ol' bloke," Abuelita's
tiny voice rasped as I twisted the bottle cap.

the picket fence

sunbleached splintered pickets
   hanging by rusty nails
   to what is left

ancient broken men
   hanging by heart beats
   to what is left

four old men

they cursed and spit and smoked
   roll-your-owns
they sat on a bench in front
   of the barber shop
they moved as slow as the revolving
   pole above them
four old men sitting in the shade
   in the heat of noon

Tano and Jimmy and Joe

Tano and Jimmy and Joe
three barbers
in white shirts

combs and scissors
clicking
electric razors
buzzing
straight razors scraping

discuss Lydia's fifth
marriage
the causes of polio
full-proof cures for colds

disagree about which year
was hottest
which the coldest
claiming
experience as proof

wax eloquent
about
Franklin Delano
"Give-'em-Hell Harry"
or "Ike"
jobs
and economy the measure

argue about baseball's best
Stan the Man
Dimaggio
or Boston's Ted
spouting
statistics to back a choice
so
why
does each always have to ask "Who's next?"

Señor Mr. Fixit

skinny as a vine

railroad cap
coke bottle glasses

whiskers

apron full of nails
hammer
hanging from a loop

metal tape measure
which he
applied to everything

el Señor Willie Mr. Fixit

at the annual church
bazaar
he built
booths for bingo
baseball throw
ring toss
pie throw
counters for food

he built shelves
for the store
cabinets in our kitchen

fixed our roof
our gate
the handle on the shovel

if I were God
I would choose him for Noah
at least
I wouldn't have to teach him
about cubits, pitch, and gopher wood

the day his athritic
hands
couldn't hold
the hammer
he asked to be buried
in his railroad cap
glasses
apron full of nails
hammer
and metal tape

he died
on the Feast of St. Joseph
patron saint
of carpenters
three days
after the church bazaar

on the day of the funeral
I stayed after
to see them fill in the grave

he's in heaven

I know

because
when I put my ear
to the ground
I heard
hammering inside the coffin

Felina

Look at that window where the light
is flickering, Manolito.
Can you see Felina's shadow
on the window shade?
Can you see the devil's shadow,
the horns and tail of Satanás?
That's her bedroom.
They dance by candlelight.

She is a witch. Es una bruja.
Hay que cuidar el mal ojo,
and don't cut through her yard.
If she sees you, she will chase you
and scream porquerías until your face
gets red and starts to turn into a devil's.

She thinks the priest sends
people to steal her santos, her books,
her money, and her roosters.
Es una viejita, but she can run fast.
Si te pesca, she will turn you
into a black rooster.
You will have to become her lover.

Yesterday, just before dark,
I went into her yard to get my baseball
by the gallinero.
I didn't think she would see me,
But she did. She called me a puto
desgraciado, and she hollered,
"¡Chingadito vienes a robar mis gallos.
Si te pesco, te haré mi gallo!"
She chased me with a broom, bruja con
escoba, and I could feel my face
turning red. Gracias a Dios I got under
the fence before I looked like the devil!

The other day, her brother from Belén
came to visit. He couldn't wake her up,
so he called the priest and the ambulance.

When the priest sprinkled agua bendito
on her, she opened her eyes, and when she
saw him, she yelled, "¿Qué estás
haciendo aquí? ¡Vete, cabrón, ladrón!"
The priest's face started to turn red,
but he crossed himself real fast and left.
Felina got out of bed and chased everyone
out of the house. Even her brother.

That was the day I saw the candles,
the santos, the black book, and the table
that looked like an altar for Mass
in her bedroom. The black book was open
on the altar. It had strange words,
not English and not Spanish. One of the
letters was as big as almost half the page.
It looked like an S. It was red and gold,
and it looked like a curved snake
with a devil's face at the bottom.
Manolito, I got real scared because
it looked like Satanás was looking right
at me from the book. I ran out faster
than the people Felina was chasing.

Every night I sit here and look at the strange
lights coming from her bedroom window.
She lights velitas to Satanás, and she makes
love to him and to her black roosters.
See? You can tell by the shadows!
Sometimes you can hear the love sounds
way over here. Tía Alicia said that she
never sees Felina at church. Tío Benito
said that's because witches who go into
churches turn into piles of dust.
Dios nos bendiga, Manolito, I hope
Satanás didn't see me from the book.

to a coal miner

no foot, no hoof, no wheel
lifts black dust
from coal mine floor
to grit and grime and gunk
your lungs

not now

now your effort
to breathe
causes
heavy lids to close
in hope of precious sleep

but when you sleep
the demon sounds
of cracking rock
and tortured wheels
whirl into twisting storms
that tear back and forth
across the floor
of your fevering brain

uncovering layers of dust
from a body
lying face up,
forcing it to rise,
the mouth to cough
black dust,
the eyes to well tears
that wash down coal-crust
cheeks, white rivers,
revealing your own face,
frightened eyes staring
into your own

until the storm ceases,
the body crumples,
the coughed dust settles,

layer upon layer,
a thick black veil,
sorrowful
shroud, over you

"Holy Mary!"
you gasp as you awaken

Pascual

at Easter Mass
Pascual
knelt on one knee
at the back of the church
as was
customary
among men in those days

he belonged to
Los Caballeros del Agnus Dei
represented
by the Lamb of God
tranfixed
with a sword
embossed in gold
on a red ribbon
worn over the pocket of the left lapel

Pascual's birthday!

he bowed his head respectfully
as the celebrant
proclaimed
the Resurrection
then intoned the Alleluia

but Pascual was reminded
of another Alleluia
the one at La Paloma Bar
on Holy Saturday
when he began an early celebration
of his birthday
by bolting down a boilermaker
first the shot
then three consecutive gulps
of ice-cold beer
blurring tears and the "Ahhh!"
of satisfaction
expressed the Alleluia aboil within

after wiping beer from chin
and tears from cheek
shot glass
and beer glass were filled again

"This one's on me!"
the cantinero announced

soon all the patrons
Caballeros del Agnus Dei
bolted down their own Alleluias
and
congratulated Pascual
with many another
before they all passed out

that was Holy Saturday

on Easter Sunday
the patrons
were all present at Mass

Pascual!
Caballeros del Agnus Dei!

that was some

resurrection

Alleluia! Alleluia! Alleluia!

Nehi Strawberry Down-and-Away

When the NEHI Strawberry pop bottle cap
curved down and away
just below the blur
of your reaching broomstick bat,
I knew I had you.

"Strike One!"

Eugene yelled from his seat on an orange crate
a few feet behind the plate,

but you stood there unruffled
and dug in for the next pop bottle cap,
your bat swinging back and forth just before
you cocked it, elbows up, behind your right ear.

I bent down and reached
into the bucket of bottle caps beside the mound.

One NEHI Strawberry left,
kept for just the right moment.

So I selected a 7-Up up-and-in
since I knew you were expecting
the RC Cola low-and-just-barely-outside.

You were creeping up on the plate.

I did my Satchel Paige loose-and-lanky wind-up
and
handcuffed you up-and-in on the wrists.

"Strike Two!"

Eugene yelled, and this time you stood there
dumbfounded,
bat never leaving your shoulder.

Then that Babe Ruth insolence crossed your face,
but I could see worry in your eyes.
Would it be the NEHI Strawberry?

I reached into the bucket
and took the Coca-Cola down-and-in.

If you didn't offer,
I'd come back with the Orange Crush
pull-the-string-and-break-your-silly-back.

You didn't,
so I concentrated on the Orange Crush
with the count at one and two.

Boy, did I pull the string!

But it landed plop at your feet
bringing the count to two and two.

I saw your eyes gleam
with new confidence, and you could
hardly wait for the next pitch.

You stared at me,
I stared at you, but I mouthed
NEHI Strawberry
To shake you up a bit.

I reached out for the NEHI Strawberry,
but my fingers closed on the NEHI Rootbeer.

I knew you'd never forgive me
if I got you with that.

I let it fly, but as I let it go, I realized I didn't
go underhand.

Your wrists snapped!

WHAP!

The cap zipped past my ear,
stinging the air,
then clattering on pavement clear across the street.

A line drive home run!

You danced like an Indian warrior,
whooping and yelling,
beating the plate with the broomstick.

Then you stopped and pointed a haughty finger
out over the center field fence
while I stood there, head down, dejected,
staring at the NEHI Strawberry in the bucket.

Tomás

Mamá. Go see for yourself.
Puro had babies. He's under the porch.
Listen. You can hear them from here.
I wonder how many.
I can hardly wait to give them names.

Santo niño, Tomás.
Puro can't have babies. He's a he.
Además, es un perro, and dogs
Can't have kittens. Only las gatas.
Que imaginación tiene este niño.

But Mamá, it's true.

Tomás, if you tell lies,
Your tongue will turn into a snake's,
Como dice in la sagrada biblia
Cuando Adán mordió la manzana en Edén.

Pero Mamá . . .

And no one will believe you when you
Have to tell the truth.
El niño Jesús never told lies,
And he made his mother very happy.

But Mamá, you can hear them from here,
And, anyway, the priest told a big lie
At church on Sunday. He told the people
That baby Jesus was born of a virgin.
Everybody still believes him.

Ay, Tomás. Go name the kittens.

Niño

With worn discolored towel
Coped over his tiny shoulders,
A child of seven circles
His house in High Mass ceremony,
Dips his fingers into an open jar
And, priest-like, arcs holy water
Onto hot, dry adobe walls.
The fragrance of fresh-wet earth
Blends strangely with the
Child's shrill chant of exorcism:

"En el nombre del Padre—¡Salte Satanás!
Y del Hijo—¡Afuera diablo!
Y del Espiritú Santo—¡Salga Satanás!"

And together dare inspire a hope
That discord might depart that house.

"Porque se mete el diablo en la pared."
His grandmother taught him.
"Y allí siembra males que crecen y entran
Por la noche en los pensamientos de la familia."

The child believes her, and why not?
Vile curses,
Strident quarrels,
And drunken accusations
Often thrust their violence
Through his bedroom wall
To worry the night
And drive deep into his desperate sleep.

He knows
The devil has sown discord.
He knows
It has infected both mother and father.
So all the more fervently
He dips fingers into the open jar
And with one motion arcs water and chant
Into the air toward the wall.

But

As he ages,
The cope falls,
The chant fades,

And the jar sits
Empty
Somewhere
In that infected house.

My Neighbor

doesn't know who she is

skeletal figure in gray gown
sitting
hour after hour
rigid
at edge of iron bed

hands that once shaped
her world
lie
palms down
one atop the other
veined stone in gray of lap

eyes that gently inspired
me
with radiant laughter
stare feebly
inward
at memories
recognizing little
trying to focus on a child's
face
spinning within a tire swing
hanging
from a cottonwood branch

cottonwood
reminding her of leaf
shadows
quaking on pink adobe
and blue shutters

heart catching at the toss
of hair
in the sun just below the window

focus
disrupted by almost understanding

2

she often called
me the neighborhood clown
so I approach her Groucho style
fingers
tapping ashes from an imaginary cigar

"The secret word, Petrita,
hanging
from the duck!
Do you know what it is?"

my eyebrows move rapidly
up and down
as I
look into her eyes for a response

the stone softens

fingers
hint at movement

eyes
slowly express recognition
but move

past
my pseudo-Groucho face
to her image
in the dresser mirror

53

where lips form
a weak smile
and
a moth of a voice flutters

"Petrita, Mr. Quack, Petrita."

eyes seeing eyes
in the mirror
laugh in a moment of knowing

roll-your-own

the gentleman steps from the porch

sheepskin coat
cowboy hat
battered boots

eighty-five
hacking cough

on his daily walk to Ben's Grocery
object
pouch of Bull Durham
extra paper
box of matches
master of the roll-your-own

back on the porch
in favorite
straight-back chair
tobacco
from pouch into flimsy paper
result
cigarette for flare of match

satisfying draw
smile on lips
curling smoke from nose and mouth
beneath
brim of hat
now downward swirl across contented face

cigarette a nub

rattle deep in chest
dry cough
contentment now discomfort
hands to coat pocket
for the makings
of a gentleman's medicine for gasping lungs

Petrita (akin to "My Neighbor")

Petrita sentada a la orilla
de su cama
ni se mueve ni parece respirar

una piedra a la orilla de un risco

me dicen que ya no pasa
la sangre
por las venas
que ya no reconoce
caras presente
ni las
caras de sus queridos

yo

su cariño payaso
su vecino
su portador de comestibles
vengo a visitar
a ver si me reconoce

yo

con cara
de Groucho

puro grande entre dedos

cara a cara
le
pregunto

"¿Me conoces, Petrita, me reconoces?"

ni movimiento de pestaña
"¿La palabra secreta, Petrita, la
que cai con el pato?
¿Me conoces, ahora, Petrita?"

ni movimiento de boca

"Mira, voy a chupar el puro
y mira como cae
la ceniza en el suelo
cuando le doy
un golpecito con los dedos."

ni respiro

ningún movimiento
esta piedra a la orilla de la cama

pero
al fin
ella en voz baja

"Señor Graznido, por favor, déjame en paz."

Fiat Lux

Fidel Adonicio Iglesias at St. Francis

Each morning of every day for thirty years
You woke up the priest
Put on a white surplice over black cassock
Rang the Angelus
Laid out priestly vestments in the sacristy
Prepared cruets of water and wine
Placed the chalice and host and missal on the altar

All for Daily Mass

All in the
Dim flicker of votive flames and sanctuary lamp

Then you shuffled up a side aisle
To the back of the church
Where you unlocked the doors for the faithful
Ladies in black shawls
Who crossed themselves with holy water
Genuflected with respect
Towards the Blessed Sacrament
Then settled into accustomed places
Eyes devout
While you moved along the opposite aisle
Stopping at each
Of several switches on the wall
Your lips forming "Fiat Lux" at every click

Each morning of every day for thirty years

Not today

This morning the miracle of automation
Rang the Angelus
The lights switched on without your "Fiat Lux"
At exactly 6:25

But no women appeared in the pews
And
Mass got started thirty minutes late

A Novice among Professionals

in the dark half hour before
the morning Angelus,
votive flames and sanctuary lamp
barely illuminate
the bowed head of Jesus crucified
hanging above the altar

a dozen women and one child
kneel
eyes
filled with sweet sadness
focused
on his immense pain
each woman praying Aves
as fingers
proceed from bead to bead

the child listens to her grandmother's
Aves,

listens to the soft whistle she emits
each time
she whispers, "de tu vientre Jesús"

listens to the drone of multiple Aves
from the women around her

listens to the methodic clack
of well-worn
rosaries against back of wooden pew

thinking they're trying to get Jesus
to look up to heaven

so
she helps with exaggerated whisper
exaggerated clack

but
somehow a five-year-old's efforts
at such ritual
causes
consternation among professionals

eyes
turn from the crucified
and
stare reprimandingly

sweet sadness turns sour
and
lips begrudge time from prayer
to express
annoyance with a novice

but
her grandmother
reaches out and embraces the child
and
whispers
"Bendita tu eres entre todas las mujeres, mi 'jita."

Botella

Vito Valdez era un molino de viento,
un windmill we say in English,
long arms in constant motion.
Ramona Ramos, cinco años his senior,
era su sweetheart, his novia we say
in Spanish, a jack-in-the-box of a lady,
always popping up
to get this, get this, get that, get that.

You could find Vito at Ramona's house
for breakfast, for lunch, for supper,
pero in return he had to fix this, fix that.
In the U.S. Navy he learned to be a cook,
so he gave Ramona advice
on liquid spices that go along with food.

He recommended un shot de bourbon
in his morning cafecito,
"Good to get el corazón to pomping,"
decía, so Ramona kept a botella just for that.

He recommended a jigger of vodka in his juice.
"Good to get el seso to thinking,"
decía, so Ramona kept a botella just for that.

He advised a dash of rum in his Coca-Cola.
"Good to get las piernas to walking,"
decìa, so Ramona kept a botella just for that.

He liked a cup of lager in his chile verde.
"Good to get las manos to grasping,"
decía, so Ramona kept a botella just for that.

They were like two cacajuetes in a shell,
but Vitorio could get cranky,
and she could be ever so demanding
with her fix this, fix this, fix that, fix that.

On a cranky day, Ramona demanded
Vito change the aceite in her Chevrolet.

El mismo día que she ran out of bourbon
por el corazón.

The very day que she ran out of vodka
for the seso.

El mismo día que she ran out of rum
por las piernas.

The very day que she ran out of lager
for the manos.

Not much motion in el windmill that day.

With well-chosen cuss words-English
and Spanish and Spanglish-he drained
the aceite, changed the filter, poured
five quarts of cheap refined, then slammed
the hood to let Ramona know he was done.

He went into la cocina to wash his manos
when he saw two wine glasses,
a botella de la best champagne,
y una nota con pretty flores which read,
"Una botella kept especially for old cranks."

He washed his manos, popped the cork,
filled las dos glasses, sipped one con gusto,
and said, "Ramona, gracias. Ven.
I'm so glad you keep un bottle just for that."

Bread Pudding

When it came to bread pudding, estas mujeres
were A-1. Ganaron el blue ribbon
at the church bazaar mas años que even Euclid
could count. They took turns winning the prize,
un año la Nora, el otro la Mercy, y casi nadie
in between. La Nora lived on East Street,
down by los trakes. La Mercy lived on Cromwell,
over by la acequia. La Nora called her bread pudding
sopa, while La Mercy called hers *capirotada*.
Toda la gente would die to have their recipes,
and on top of that, they didn't trust each other.

Un año cuando La Nora tuvo sixty y La Mercy
tuvo cincuenta y cinco años de edad, someone
else won the contest. That someone era Adelino,
the one who delivered groceries for the store.
La Nora era his tía on his jefe's side,
while La Mercy was his mother's oldest sister.
When he delivered groceries, le invitaban into
la casa since he was familia. They offered him
un cafecito y un biscochito and sometimes
even some bread pudding, sopa at La Nora's
and capirotada at La Mercy's. Mmmmm good.

Y since Adelino siempre hablaba de hacerse
un baker, they revealed some of their recipes
if he made una promesa al señor Jesucristo
not to tell. After all, he was familia. But they
never told him the one for the bread pudding.

Las dos mujeres ordered special a few days
before the contest, so Adelino learned about
the ingredients, just not how much, what order,
what temperature, ni how long to let it bake.

Rainbow bread, one day old, slightly toasted
or left out overnight, he guessed. Kraft longhorn
cheddar, graded thinly in two or three piles,
he thought. Del Monte brand raisins. Two scoops?
C & H white cane sugar, enough to sweeten.
Schilling cinnamon, sprinkled from the largest can.
Bacardi rum. And here's the main difference.
When it came to the evaporated milk, La Nora
ordered Pet while La Mercy insisted on Carnation.

Un año the grocery store ran out of Pet and Carnation,
so Adelino sent cada mujer un brand differente
for free. That's the year Adelino gano la blue ribbon
for un bread pudding superb which he called *sopirotada*.

Encounter with La Llorona
upon His Return from Harvard

late October's moonlight
chill casts
a gray-white mist
upon the day's
vibrant red and gold
of brush
along the river's banks

like an Aeneas
he stands
at the edge of Tartarus
expecting to see Charon
standing silently
in his boat beckoning to those
who would cross
holding
his boney hand out
for the penny

like Aeneas
he thinks of turning
to Sybil for protection
from the hidden
crouching three-throated dog

not since he
was ten had he walked
this way on Halloween
and never alone

for he had heard it said
that those souls
whose bodies were never
retrieved

from the river's bottom
that lie entangled
in roots along the river's edge
haunt these banks
called forth
by the moon's eerie chill

he does not know
what called him here
or why he came alone
for he knew that anyone
who happened
upon a soul rising from
the river is rooted
to the bank
must observe hideous
transformations
is in danger of losing his soul

he tried to turn
and run from that place
but too late
for a mist spiraled
from the river's surface
an El Greco figure
enlongating towards the moon

clouding it
becoming the face of a woman
in pain
hollowed eyes
and wailing mouth

the moon
becoming two
a cold pupil in each hollow
staring
directly into his own
searching
for his soul
trying to suck it forth

in that moment of panic
he remembered what
the old one's taught
about fighting off these
restless souls

he forced his eyes shut
and cried out

"Señora I am not yours

your children
have long been swept away
though their souls
may wander
somewhere along the shore

Señora I am not yours"

the pull subsided
as the mist's chill grip
released him

he opened his eyes
and
saw only hollows
where
the moon's had been

the mist
uncovered the moon
and
spiraled down
shortening in length
until it returned
to the river

leaving him alone

Elifás

no lo conecería
sin
pipa en la boca
este
cliente de la tienda

siempre
entra con la misma
pregunta

"¿Cuánto cuesta
el Sir Walter Raleigh
y
el Prince Albert?"

y para quejarse que
no vendemos tabaco
con
nombre de caballero español

un día dejó la pipa
sobre
el mostrador

la cogí
la examiné
y
cuando volvió a coger la pipa
le dije
"Esta pipa barata es de Inglaterra"

se me 'nojó

outcast grave

just outside
the wrought-iron fence
at the Catholic cemetary
stands a four-foot cross

splintered plywood nailed
to weathered pine

it marks a sand-and-gravel
grave
and bears the inscription
R.I.P.
in what seems like red nail polish
right where
the I.N.R.I. should be

but it doesn't name who or when

just below
the cross beam
someone fastened
an eight-inch-tall plastic corpus

a glow-in-the-dark type
I believe
taken
trom some dime-store crucifix

fastened not with nails
but three
long-stemmed tacks
one in each hand
and one through crossed feet

the wire stem
of a crepe-paper poppy
pierces

the wound in its side
as though it were a button hole
on a gentleman's lapel

attached
not long ago
judging from the green
on the stem
and the red in the blossom

who is buried here?

I don't know

but
he or she
must have done a grievous wrong

I meant only
to pass
this way
but
now I think I'll stay to see

if the corpus glows in the dark

Carmela

Cada miércoles, "Double Stamp Day," Carmela
entraba de compras en silla rodante
acompañada por su enfermera, la Señora Brown.

Viéndola siempre me espantaba porque Carmela
casi podía hablar,
casi podía levantar las manos para domonstrar
lo que quería comprar.
Por eso siempre nos entregaba una lista.

El dueño siempre le abría la puerta, y tomando
Sus manos en las suyas, decía,
"Me alegro mucho verte, Carmela. A tu servicio."

Carmela respondía con un solo, "Haaloo."

Al fin de las compras, la dueña la cumplimentaba
sobre el color de su vestido y le daba una
banda para el cabello que casaba bien con el vestido.

Los dueños y la Señora Brown siempre se burlaban de mí,
Diciendo que la Carmen estaba enamorada de mí.

Un miércoles no estaban los dueños. Entraron Carmela
y la Señora Brown. ¡Aye, Dios! ¿Qué iba hacer?

Abrí la puerta. Dije, "Me da mucho gusto verte,
Carmela," pero no pude tomar sus manos en las mías
porque temblaban como dos terremotos gigantes.

Y cuando acabaron de compras, como la dueña, le
dije que me gustaba el color de su vestido,
pero luego no supe cual color de banda se casaba
bien con su vestido. Viendo mi desconcierto,
Carmela extendió sus manos a las mías
con dificultad y con dificultad dijo, "Rohoh."

The Lord's Day at the Grocery Store

meant
washing out the meat counter
taking
hanks of meat from the freezer beneath
removing
display trays from above
using
rubber gloves
scrapers
buckets of hot water
and a ton of rags
to attack
frozen suet and frozen puddles of blood
then
washing display windows and counter
with a vinegar solution
inside and out
to make smell good what smelled bad

then the floor

sweeping sawdust into dust pans
scrapers
buckets of hot water
and three or four mops
then
when dry
spreading fresh sawdust in preparation
for six days of work

the priest told us it's a sin to work on God's
day of rest
but I told him God don't work at Ben's store

Spearmint Whistle

The shop whistle blew each workday at four
in the afternoon, filling the desert air and
signaling the egress of crowds of workmen
in overalls and engineer caps through a gate
in a tall wooden fence that separated
the Santa Fe Railroad yards from East Street.

Four city blocks away, at a home near the
grocery store, a brown-eyed child of five
dressed in short pants swung back and forth
on a squeaky, springy wooden gate. He was
waiting to catch a glimpse of his father,
lunch bucket in hand, walking up the street.

Each workman took an accustomed path home.
The boy waited every afternoon for his father's
familiar shape, starting his wait after an hour nap,
each wait resulting in a piece of candy, a cookie,
or a stick of Spearmint Gum which his father,
a Houdini, pulled from his empty lunch bucket.

Today the gum appeared. The boy hurried to
unwrap it, but it wouldn't unwrap. It was metal.
A trick? Disappointed, he kicked up dirt, but
his father took the gum, put it to his own mouth,
and made it whistle. "Here's how you do it,
Celino," and from that moment on Celino drove

The neighbors, people in the street, at the store
at the barbershop, and outside the church crazy
with a monotone of "Three Blind Mice."
One day he forgot to take the whistle out of his
pocket, so it broke when his mother washed the
pants and put them through the wringer. Celino
cried, thinking his father would be very angry.

His father simply said, "Those things happen,"
and left it at that. The next day he waited, hoping
his father would bring home another whistle,
after all, he was Houdini. When his father
saw Celino swinging on the fence, he put down
his lunch bucket, opened it, and showed him
Him a stick of gum at the bottom. Celino
reached for it, lifted it to his lips. Real gum?
His face fell. He threw it in the dirt. He turned
his back. Afraid of his father's anger, Celino
bent to pick up the gum and say, "I'm sorry,"
but in its place was a Spearmint Gum whistle.

Boiled Ham

when we worked on Sundays
Ben always let us
make sandwiches for when we got hungry
and we did
our favorite being minced ham and Royal Crown Cola
and peanuts
to make the soda fizz in the bottle

that's until we discovered boiled ham which cost
twice as much for the customer
and
the bottle of Jack Daniels hiding in the storeroom
which made us happy with it in the Royal Crown Cola

one day Ben caught us eating the boiled ham
and
drinking the Jack Daniels in the Royal Crown Cola

yelled "You guys aren't old enough to"—but seeing
his wife Irene come in and pushing the Jack
Daniels under an apron—"to eat the boiled ham!

Translation Notes

Only words and phrases that cannot be understood from the context are
translated.

"Gloria"

Gloria in excelsis Deo--Latin "Glory to God in the highest"
. . . et in terra pax hominibus--Latin ". . . and on earth peace to all
mankind."

"buscando la gloria eterna" not translated since "It is morning", p. 9, is a rendition
of that poem.

"Telemo"

Ruega por míTelemo, ahora y en la hora de mi muerte--Pray for me
Telemo, now and at the hour of my death.
Lo siento mucho--I feel (your suffering) greatly.
Me acuerdo cuando to mamá--I remember when your mother.
Dios te ayude--May God help you.
Lupe . . . mujer de paciencia--Lupe . . . woman of patience.
cuando,Odiséo, su papá, deserted *la famila*--when his father, Odysseus,
deserted the family.
un vagamundo--a hobo (wanderer)
y en voz conocido ruega, "Telemo, por favor, un frajo para Odiséo--in a
familiar voice he begs, "Telemo, a cigarette for Odysseus, please.

"Adán"

¿Y porqué?--And why?
el mismo diablo--the devil himself
chingazos--derogatory term for coming to blows with fists
bolsa--hip pocket in this context
traguitos--sips, little swallows
un lugar along the *acequia*--a place along the irrigation ditch
los pájaros--the birds
pelear con los bushes--fight with the bushes
bajo la puente--under the bridge
otra vez con cariño--again with loving care
parasol en la mano--umbrella in hand
la mano izquierda--the left hand
al mismo tiempo--at the same time
se acuerda de eso otro Adán--he remembers that other Adam
todo el mundo--the whole world

"Mario Martinez"

Con verguenza, siempre esperando--with shame, always waiting
(hoping)
pero nadie esta allí--but no one is there
espera--he waits

77

"Santos"

pinche--derogatory term
un traguito--a sip, a little swallow
ese--that
Hijo--means son, but used as "gosh," "goodness," etc.
la viejita--little old lady
Mira--Look
Oye--Listen, Hey
No te importa--It's none of your business
Palo--means stick, but here Pow! Ouch!

"La Señal de la Cruz"

La Señal de la Cruz--The Sign of the Cross
con un brazo, el derecho, / El izquierdo / Pero--with one arm, the right one, / The left one / But
gallinas--chickens
una noche--one night

"Milagro entre Comestibles"

means miracle among the groceries--the rest not translated since it is a rendition "Annie"

"Back Then"

era para el owner if *la jura*--for the owner if the police
Pero si tuvieras--But if you had
cordón . . . campanita--string . . . little bell
¡Órale, José, aquí esta . . .--Hey, Jose, Mr. Lincoln is here. He wants in.
que Alquien--for someone

"Genes"

"De tal palo tal astilla"--from such a stick such a splinter
Abuelita--little grandmother
mi jefito--my dad, i.e. my little chief
que duro era--how hard it was
descalzo--barefoot
nieve--snow
Ayer--yesterday
Mi'jita--my daughter, more at my little darling
pendejo--idiot

"Felina"

Hay que cuidar el mal ojo--One must look out for the evil eye
Porquerías--dirty words
Es una viejita--she's an old lady
Si te pesca--if she catches you
gallinero--the hen house

puto desgraciado--derogatory phrase, something like disgraceful male whore

¡Chingadito vienes a robar mis gallow. / Si te pesco, te haré mi gallo!-- Something like "You little brat coming to steal my roosters, / if I catch you, I will make you my rooster," but stronger.

¿Qué estas haciendo aquí?--What are you doing here?

¡Vete, cabrón, ladrón!--Get out of here you goat (derogatory), thief!

Dios nos bendiga--May God bless us

"Tomas"

Puro--play on words, the dog's name, but the word means cigar or pure.

Santo niño--Holy Child

Además--furthermore

Que imaginación tiene este niño--What an imagination this child has

Como dice en la sagrada biblila / Cuando Adán mordió la manzana en Edén--As it says in the Holy Bible / When Adam bit the apple in Eden.

"Pascual"

Pascual--Easter, but also the name of an individual

Los Cabelleros del Agnus Dei--a society of men who serve the church in various capacities: The Gentlemen of the Lamb of God

"Niño"

"En el nombre del Padre . . . (three lines)--In the name of the Father-- Satan, depart! / And of the Son--Out Devil? / And of the Holy Spirit-- Get out Satan!

Porque se mete el diablo en la pared--For the devil gets into the wall.

Y allí siembra males que crecen y entran / Por la noche en los Pensamientos de la familia--and there he (the devil) plants seeds that enter the thoughts of the family.

"Petrita" (rough translation)

Petrita seated at the end of her bed does not move nor does she appear to breathe

a stone on the edge of a cliff

they tell me that her blood no longer passes through her veins, that she no longer recognizes present faces or the faces of her loved ones
I

her beloved clown, her neighbor, her deliverer of groceries, come to visit to see if she recognizes me

I

with Groucho's face

with a large cigar in my fingers

face to face I ask her

"Don't you know me, don't you recognize me?"

not even the movement of an eyelash

"The secret word, Petrita, the one the duck carries? Do you recognize me now?"

no movement of the mouth

"Look, I am going to puff on the cigar, see how the ash falls to the floor when I
tap it with my fingers"

no breath

not a single movement from this stone at the edge of the bed
but finally in a low voice

"Mr. Quack, please leave me alone"

"Elifás"

I wouldn't know this client of the store without a pipe in his mouth

he always enters (the store) with the same question

"How much does Sir Walter Raleigh and Prince Albert cost?"

and to complain that we don't sell tobacco with a Spanish gentleman's name

one day he left his pipe on the counter

I picked it up, examined it, and when he came back for the pipe, I said, "This is a cheap English pipe!"

he got mad

"Fiat Lux"

> *Fiat lux*--Latin "Let there be light."

"A Novice among Professionals"

> *Bendita tu eres entre todas la mujeres, mi'jita*--"Blessed art thou among all women, my darling child (here a granddaughter)."

"Bread Pudding"

> *estas mujeres*--these women
> *Ganaron*--won
> *Un año la Nora, el otro La Mercy, y casi nadie*--one year Nora , the other year Mercy, and hardly anyone in between
> *años de edad*--years of age (Nora was sixty, Mercy was fifty-five)

"Carmela" (rough translation)

> Every Wednesday, Double Stamp Day, Carmela, seated in wheel chair, came to the store to buy groceries, accompanied by Mrs. Brown.
>
> Seeing her always frightened me because Carmela could hardly speak or lift her hands to point out what she wanted to buy. That's why she gave us a list.
>
> The owner always held the door open for her, and taking her hands in his, said, "I am so happy to see you, Camela. I am at your service."
>
> Carmela simply answered, "Haaloo."
>
> When she finished shopping, the owner's wife complimented her on the color of her dress and gave her a matching ribbon for her hair. The owners and Mrs. Brown always teased me, saying that Carmela was in love with me.
>
> One Wednesday the owners were away. Carmela and Mrs. Brown Came to the store. Oh, Lord! What was I going to do?
>
> I opened the door. I said, "I am so happy to see you, Carmela." But I couldn't hold her hands because mine were trembling like two giant earthquakes.
>
> And when they finished shopping, I did just as the owner's wife. I told her how pretty her dress was, but then I was at a loss as to what color ribbon would match her dress. Seeing my discomfort, Carmela reached for my hands with difficulty, and with difficulty said, "Red."